I AM
WHO
THE BIBLE
SAYS
I AM

I Am Summary

In the book of Genesis, after Adam and Eve disobeyed God and ate from the tree of knowledge of good and evil, they hid from God.

When God called out to Adam, Adam said he hid because He was afraid when he discovered he was
naked. And God asked him "who told you you were na-ked?" (Genesis 2:25-3:11).

So, who told you that you are _____?
That blank represents anything and everything God has NOT said about you.

Instead of accepting what the enemy has told you (through society, culture, family, bosses, even the
voices in your head), we should instead embrace the truth found in God's Word.

In this resource, we share 50 powerful truths about who God made us to be as found in the bible. Make
these your regular declarations and become the person God already made you to be.

"The only place we will find ourselves
is in the word of God."
~Pastor Mike Freeman

I *Am*
made in God's image

Then God said, "Let Us make man in Our image, according to Our likeness; let them have dominion over the fish of the sea, over the birds of the air, and over the cattle, over all the earth and over every creeping thing that creeps on the earth."

So God created man in His own image; in the image of God He created him; male and female He created them.

Genesis 1:26-27 NKJV

Reflection

I *Am*

called by God's name

Your words were found, and I ate them, And Your word was to me the joy and rejoicing of my heart; For I am called by Your name, O Lord God of hosts.

Jeremiah 15:16 NKJV

Reflection

I *Am*
wonderfully complex

Thank you for making me so wonderfully complex! Your workmanship is marvelous-how well I know it.

Psalms 139:14 NLT

Reflection

I *Am*
God's masterpiece

For we are God's masterpiece. He has created us anew in Christ Jesus, so we can do the good things he planned for us long ago.

Ephesians 2:10 NLT

Reflection

I *Am*
the apple of God's eye

Keep me as the apple of Your eye;
Hide me under the shadow of Your wings.

Psalms 17:8 NKJV

Reflection

I *Am*
loved

God so loved the world that he gave his one and only Son. Anyone who believes in him will not die but will have eternal life.

John 3:16 NIRV

Learn More:
1 John 4:9-11

Reflection

I *Am*
a child of god

For you are all children of God through faith in Christ Jesus.

Galatians 3:26 NLT

Learn More:
John 1:12; Romans 8:14-17; Psalms 82:6

Reflection

I *Am*
a heir of God's promise

And [if] you belong to Christ if you are in [Him"], then you are Abraham's descendants, and

[spiritual"] heirs according to [God's] promise.

Galatians 3:29 AMP

Learn More:
Galatians 3:7-9; Romans 8:14-17

Reflection

I *Am*
anointed

I am anointed with fresh oil [for Your service].
Psalms 92:10 AMP

Learn More:
Psalms 23:5; Psalms 45:7; 1 Samuel 10:1

Reflection

I *Am*
ordained

Ye have not chosen me, but I have chosen you, and ordained you, that ye should go and bring forth fruit, and that your fruit should remain: that whatsoever ye shall ask of the Father in my name, he may give it you

John 15:16 KJV

Reflection

I *Am*
a leader and not a follower

The Lord your God will make you leaders, not followers. Pay attention to his commands that I'm giving you today. Be careful to obey them. Then you will always be on top. You will never be on the bottom.

Deuteronomy 28:13 NIRV

Reflection

I *Am*
a saint and not a sinner

[I am writing] to all who are beloved of God in Rome, called to be saints [God's people] and set apart for a sanctified life, [that is, set apart for God and His purpose].

Romans 1:7a AMP

Learn More:
Psalms 34:9 AMP

Reflection

I *Am*

God's chosen

But you are a chosen people, a royal priesthood, a holy nation, God's special possession, that you may declare the praises of him who called you out of darkness into his wonderful light.

1 Peter 2:9 NIV

Learn More:
Colossians 3:12; 1 Peter 1:2; Ephesians 1:3-5

Reflection

I *Am*

a member of the body of Christ

Now you [collectively] are Christ's body, and individually [you are] members of it [each with its own special purpose and function].

1 Corinthians 12:27 AMP

Learn More:
Romans 12:4-5; Ephesians 5:30

Reflection

I *Am*
a servant of God

[I am] a servant of God and the Lord Jesus Christ.

James 1:1a ERV

Learn More:
John 15:12-17

Reflection

I *Am*
a friend of God

Jesus said you are My friends if you do whatever I command you. No longer do I call you servants, for a servant does not know what his master is doing; but I have called you friends, for all things that I heard from My Father I have made known to you.

John 15:14-15 NKJV

Reflection

I *Am*
a king

To Him Jesus who loved us and washed our sins in His own blood, and as made us kings and priests to His God and Father, to Him be glory and dominion forever and ever. Amen.

Revelation 1:5b-6 NKJVV

Reflection

I *Am*

a royal priest

But God chose you to be his people. You are royal priests. You are a holy nation. You are God's special treasure. You are all these things so that you can give him praise. God brought you out of darkness into his wonderful light.

1 Peter 2:9 NIRV

Learn More:
1 Peter 2:5; Revelations 1:5-6

Reflection

I *Am*
the elect of God

Therefore, as the elect of God, holy and beloved, put on tender mercies, kindness, humility, meekness, longsuffering.

Colossians 3:12 NJKV

Learn More:
1 Peter 1:2; Ephesians 1:3-5; 1 Peter 2:9

Reflection

I *Am*
an ambassador for Christ

So we are ambassadors for Christ, as though God were making His appeal through us; we [as Christ's representatives] plead with you on behalf of Christ to be reconciled to God.

2 Corinthians 5:20 AMP

Reflection

I *Am*
the salt of the earth

Jesus said "You are the salt of the earth; but if the salt has lost its taste (purpose), how can it be made salty? It is no longer good for anything, but to be thrown out and walked on by people [when the walkways are wet and slippery].

Matthew 5:13 AMP

Learn More:
Mark 9:50

Reflection

I *Am*
the light of the world

Jesus said "You are the light of [Christ to] the world. A city set on a hill cannot be hidden; Let your light shine before men in such a way that they may see your good deeds and moral excellence, and [recognize and honor and] glorify your Father who is in heaven.

Matthew 5:14,16 AMP

Learn More:
Philippians 2:14-15; Proverbs 4:18; John 8:12

Reflection

I *Am*
blessed

Give praise to the God and Father of our Lord Jesus Christ. He has blessed us with every spiritual blessing. Those blessings come from the heavenly world. They belong to us because we belong to Christ.

Ephesians 1:3 NIRV

Learn More:
Psalms 1:1-3; 32:1-2; Genesis 1:28; 12:2

Reflection

I *Am*
prosperous

Beloved, I pray that you may prosper in all things and be in health, just as your soul prospers.

3 John 1:2 NKJV

Learn More:
Joshua 1:8; Psalms 1:1-3

Reflection

I *Am*
a winner (victorious)

No! In all these things we are more than winners! We owe it all to Christ, who has loved us.

Romans 8:37 NIRV

Learn More:
John 16:33; 1 Corinthians 15:57; 1 John 5:4-5

Reflection

I *Am*

an overcomer

Little children (believers, dear ones), you are of God and you belong to Him and have [already]overcome them, the [agents of the antichrist]; because He who is in you is greater than he (Satan) who is in the world [of sinful mankind].

1 John 4:4 AMP

Learn More:
John 16:33; 1 Corinthians 15:57; 1 John 5:4-5

Reflection

I *Am*
saved

For it is by grace [God's remarkable compassion and favor drawing you to Christ] that you have been saved [actually delivered from judgment and given eternal life] through faith. And this [salvation] is not of yourselves [not through your own effort], but it is the [undeserved, gracious] gift of God.

Ephesians 2:8 AMP

Learn More:
John 3:16-17

Reflection

I *Am*
reedemed

But now, this is what the Lord , your Creator says, O Jacob, And He who formed you, O Israel, "Do not fear, for I have redeemed you [from captivity]; I have called you by name; you are Mine!

Isaiah 43:1 AMP

Learn More:
Psalms 107:2; 31:5; 77:15; Lamentations 3:58

Reflection

I *Am*
forgiven

I will praise the Lord. I won't forget anything he does for me. He forgives all my sins. He heals all my sicknesses.

Psalm 103:2-3 NIRV

Learn More:
Matthew 6:12; Luke 11:4; 1 John 2:12

Reflection

I *Am*
free (from sin)

Jesus said "And you shall know the truth, and the truth shall make you free. Therefore if the Son makes you free, you shall be free indeed."

John 8:32,36 NKJV

Learn More:
Romans 8:2; Galatians 5:1

Reflection

I *Am*
righteous

[God] made Christ who knew no sin to [judicially] be sin on our behalf, so that in Him we would become the righteousness of God [that is, we would be made acceptable to Him and placed in a right relationship with Him by His gracious loving kindness].

2 Corinthians 5:21 AMP

Learn More:
Romans 3:21-23; 1 Corinthians 1:30 ERV

Reflection

I *Am*
NOT ashamed

I know that you are praying for me. I also know that God will give me the Spirit of Jesus Christ to help me. So no matter what happens, I'm sure I will still be set free. I completely expect and hope that I won't be ashamed in any way. I'm sure I will be brave enough. Now as always Christ willreceive glory because of what happens to me. He will receive glory whether I live or die.

Philippians 1:19-20 NIRV

Reflection

I *Am*
healed

Christ carried our sins in his body on the cross. He did this so that we would stop living for sin and live for what is right. By his wounds you were healed.

1 Peter 2:24 ERV

Learn More:
Isaiah 58:8; Psalms 30:2; 103:2-3; James 5:14-16

Reflection

I *Am*

in perfect health

Beloved, I pray that in every way you may succeed and prosper and be in good health [physically], just as [I know] your soul prospers [spiritually].

3 John 1:2 AMP

Learn More:
Jeremiah 30:17

Reflection

I *Am*
protected

Those who go to God Most High for safety will be protected by the Almighty. I will say to the Lord , "You are my place of safety and protection. You are my God and I trust you."

Psalms 91:1-2 NCV

Learn More:
Psalms 91

Reflection

I *Am*
delivered

Surely [God] shall deliver you from the snare of the fowler And from the perilous pestilence. "Because he has set his love upon Me, therefore I will deliver him; I will set him on high, because he has known My name. He shall call upon Me, and I will answer him; I will be with him in trouble; I will deliver him and honor him.

Psalms 91:3,14-15 NKJV

Reflection

I *Am*

at peace

Jesus says "I leave my peace with you. I give my peace to you. I do not give it to you as the world does. Do not let your hearts be troubled. And do not be afraid."

John 14:27 NIRV

Learn More:
Philippians 4:7; Colossians 3:15)

Reflection

I *Am*
comforted

Blessed be the God and Father of our Lord Jesus Christ, the Father of mercies and God of all comfort, who comforts us in all our tribulation, that we may be able to comfort those who are in any trouble, with the comfort with which we ourselves are comforted by God.

2 Corinthians 1:3-4 NKJV

Reflection

I *Am*

an imitator of God

Therefore become imitators of God [copy Him and follow His example], as well-beloved children [imitate their father].

Ephesians 5:1 AMP

Learn More:
Luke 6:36; 1 Peter 1:15-16; Matthew 5:48

Reflection

I *Am*
a god

I said, You are gods [since you judge on My behalf, as My representatives]; indeed, all of you are children of the Most High.

Psalm 82:6 AMPC

Learn More:
John 10:34-36

Reflection

I *Am*
holy

But like the Holy One who called you, be holy yourselves in all your conduct [be set apart from the world by your godly character and moral courage]; because it is written, "You shall be holy (set apart), for I am holy."

1 Peter 1:15-16 AMP

Reflection

I *Am*
perfect

You, therefore, will be perfect [growing into spiritual maturity both in mind and character, actively integrating godly values into your daily life], as your heavenly Father is perfect.

Matthew 5:48 AMP

Reflection

I *Am*
fearless

God gave us his Spirit. And the Spirit doesn't make us weak and fearful. Instead, the Spirit gives us power and love. He helps us control ourselves.

2 Timothy 1:7 NIRV

Learn More:
Romans 8:14-16; John 14:27; Psalms 23:4

Reflection

I *Am*
powerful

For God has not given us a spirit of fear, but of power and of love and of a sound mind.

2 Timothy 1:7 NKJV

Learn More:
Acts 1:8

Reflection

I *Am*
a disciple of Jesus

Then Jesus said to those Jews who believed Him, "If you abide in My word, you are My disciples indeed. And you shall know the truth, and the truth shall make you free."

John 8:31-32 NKJV

Reflection

I *Am*
Christ's

You who belong to Christ are Abraham's seed.
So you will receive what God has promised.

Galatians 3:29 NIRV

Reflection

I *Am*

God's building

For we are God's fellow workers; you are God's field, you are God's building. Do you not know that you are the temple of God and that the Spirit of God dwells in you?

I Corinthians 3:9,16 NKJV

Learn More:
1 Peter 2:5

Reflection

I *Am*

God's worker/laborer

You, therefore, will be perfect [growing into spiritual maturity both in mind and character, actively integrating godly values into your daily life], as your heavenly Father is perfect.

Matthew 5:48 AMP

Reflection

____

____

____

____

____

I *Am*
like Jesus

If God's love is made perfect in us, we can be without fear on the day when God judges the world. We will be without fear, because in this world we are like Jesus.

1 John 4:17 ERV

Learn More:
John 8:12; Matthew 5:14

Reflection

I *Am*
who I am by the grace of God

But God's amazing grace has made me who I am! And his grace to me was not fruitless. In fact, I worked harder than all the rest, yet not in my own strength but God's, for his empowering grace is poured out upon me.

1 Corinthians 15:10 TPT

Reflection

____

____

____

____

____

AS
GOD IS
SO
AM I

Become Who You Were Made to Be

The truth is we can't know who we are until we know who God is. And we can't know who God is, unless we approach Him through His Son, Jesus Christ.

Jesus is the way, the truth and the life.
No one comes to the Father except through Him
John 14:6

The bible tells us that whoever calls on the name of the Lord Jesus shall be saved. You can receive Jesus today as your Lord and Savior by confessing with your mouth and believing in your heart that Jesus Christ is the Son of God.

To do so, say the following prayer:

"Heavenly Father, I recognize that I am a sinner. I receive the free gift of eternal life by acknowledging Jesus Christ is the Son of God. I believe that He died for all my sins and was raised from the dead.
Today, I have become a new person and a child of God and my name has been written in the Lamb's Book of Life.

In Jesus name I pray. Amen."

Welcome to the kingdom of heaven!

Because of your confession, God now lives in you, and you in God.

We encourage you to develop a habit of spending time in God's Word (i.e. the bible). It is important that your mind be renewed even as your spirit has been made new. And find a good Bible-based church in your area where you can grow in your walk with God.

To start, read these scripture references on salvation to learn more about your spiritual transformation.

Romans 3:23   *2 Corinthians 5:17*
*Romans 10:9-13**Psalms 1:1-2*
Romans 12:2   *John 3:14-18*
Romans 6:23   *John 1:12-13*
Revelation 3:5   *John 14:6*

Learn more at https://biblestorm.com/salvation/

About BibleStorm

BibleStorm makes bible trivia products with one primary purpose - to illuminate hidden truth found in God's Word. As such, the foundational scripture for our business and mission is found in Psalm 119:18.

"Open my eyes [to spiritual truth]
so that I may behold Wonderful things from Your law."
Psalm 119:18 AMP

Our experience informs us that while many people may be familiar with the Bible and even encounter it on a semi-regular basis, many do not know or understand what it says. And this can have a significant negative impact in our walk with God.

"My people are destroyed because they don't know
Me" and
"lack knowledge [of My law, where I reveal My will]"
Hosea 4:6

But God has left his Word (i.e. the bible) for us to get to know Him. We believe that trivia is a fun way to (re)introduce the bible, biblical themes and concepts. Our prayer is that you develop a hunger/desire to learn more about God through His Word.